(Previous Page)

Pacific Beach • South from Crystal Pier • 1926

Cars, tents, umbrellas and scattered homes lined
Pacific Beach's ocean front in 1926. The cliff
was unprotected and it required a steep descent
to access the beach from the street above.

Photography: San Diego Historical Society

San Diego

then & now

SECOND EDITION 2001
PUBLISHED BY:
GEORGE ROSS JEZEK PHOTOGRAPHY & PUBLISHING
P.O. BOX 600253
SAN DIEGO CA 92160

WWW.SANDIEGOTHENANDNOW.COM

CONCEPT BY:
GEORGE ROSS JEZEK

PRODUCED BY:
GEORGE ROSS JEZEK

CONTEMPORARY PHOTOGRAPHY BY:
GEORGE ROSS JEZEK

WRITTEN BY:
ROGER M. SHOWLEY

ALL BLACK AND WHITE PHOTOGRAPHS ARE COURTESY OF THE
SAN DIEGO HISTORICAL SOCIETY, WITH THE FOLLOWING EXCEPTIONS:
SAN DIEGO AEROSPACE MUSEUM, POINT LOMA AERIAL PHOTO, PAGE 50
CARLSBAD CITY LIBRARY, CARLSBAD DOWNTOWN PHOTO, PAGE 90

ALL COLOR PHOTOGRAPHS © GEORGE ROSS JEZEK

ISBN 0-9701036-0-3

GRAPHIC DESIGN:
MINK GRAPHIC DESIGN

PRINTED IN HONG KONG THROUGH CREATIVE PRINT MANAGEMENT, USA

THE SAN DIEGO HISTORICAL SOCIETY MAINTAINS AN ACTIVE ARCHIVE
OF IMAGES PERTAINING TO SAN DIEGO HISTORY. FOR MORE INFORMATION
CONTACT THE SAN DIEGO HISTORICAL SOCIETY AT
P.O. BOX 81825 SAN DIEGO CA 92138
(619) 232-6203

SAN DIEGO HISTORICAL SOCIETY

© GEORGE ROSS JEZEK

This book is dedicated in memory of my mother,

Jean Dietrich Jezek.

Her encouragement, love, and devotion for San Diego inspired the undertaking of this book.

G.R.J.

Table of Contents

SAN DIEGO HISTORICAL SOCIETY

© GEORGE ROSS JEZEK

Introduction
BY ROGER M. SHOWLEY

SAN DIEGO HISTORICAL SOCIETY

Newcomers to San Diego County inevitably fall in love with the place - its beguiling climate, its varied landscape, its energetic people. But after a few years, these new residents invariably remark on how things have changed. The traffic is worse. There are too many people. Houses cost more. Throughout its history, San Diego has known this one constant — change. At times it is rapid, at others, it's slow. But always, things are different.

This book aims to restore some of that civic memory. In many pictures and few words, San Diego's past returns to remind us what once was, who lived here, what they did and built. Wipe away the present and you'll rediscover natural landscapes you never knew. Mission Valley before the freeways. Oceanside beachgoers camped on the sand. Lakeside around a lake. But curiously, some scenes have changed little over many decades. El Cortez still towers over downtown, an apartment building again, just as it once was, its 1950s "improvements" stripped away to reveal a beauty long forgotten. The Villa Montezuma in Sherman Heights is surrounded by homes and mature trees. But its Victorian glory remains revealed, a celebration of an exuberant age.

To recoup San Diego's history in pictures, George Ross Jezek started on this photographic journey in the late-1990s after attending a lecture at the Museum of Photographic Arts in Balboa Park. Born in San Diego, he knew his way around most of the county. His father, a business executive, had come here from Illinois as a naval officer during the Korean War. His mother had come about the same time to accept a teaching position after graduating from Ohio State University.

George, a graduate of Brooks Institute of Photography in Santa Barbara and a professional photographer, decided the best approach to tracing San Diego's history was to match historic photos with contemporary shots of the same locations today. From the San Diego Historical Society's extensive collection of photographs and other sources, he selected 70 representative scenes. Then he tracked down the exact location from which each historic photo was taken and captured in color the same scene as it looks now. Sometimes the task was easy, sometimes difficult, even dangerous. At times George had to wait weeks for just the right weather at the beach. At other times, he talked his way into people's backyards and buildings to access the desirable shot from which to point his camera.

Near the end of the project, George invited me to research the background of each scene and provide material for the captions. I consulted city directories, news clippings, books and magazines and conducted several interviews to describe as accurately as possible what once was. Finally, I asked Jane and Larry Booth, the retired photo archivists at the San Diego Historical Society, and Philip M. Klauber, a retired executive with an unequalled grasp of San Diego history, to review the manuscript and suggest any changes. But in many cases, few words were necessary. The pictures told their own story -- the beauty of Torrey Pines State Park, the majesty of Point Loma, the manmade wonder of Sweetwater Dam.

To the outsider, San Diego's photographed history may occupy but a few moments in time, roughly 120 years, a lifetime and a half. But it's a rich, fascinating story that many natives as well as newcomers never learn. By the time the first photo included here was taken, San Diego had already set much of its destiny. Discovered by Spaniards in 1542, settled by soldiers and priests in 1769 over the objections of the local Indian tribes, San Diego started out as a resource-poor colonial outpost on the Pacific.

Once the United States seized California in the Mexican-American War in 1846, things began to change. New arrivals imagined a great seaport, connected by rail to the east. Irrigation unlocked the region's agricultural riches. The climate beckoned health seekers who stayed at grand resorts, most notably, the Hotel Del Coronado, which opened in 1887. The great real estate boom of the 1880s gave way to a prolonged slump that relented only when the 1915-16 Panama-California Exposition in Balboa Park exposed the rest of the world to San Diego, and when World War I brought the Navy to town.

The 1920s and '30s transformed San Diego into the air capital of the west. Reuben H. Fleet moved his Consolidated Aircraft from Buffalo in 1935 and for the next 60 years, San Diego's economy was dependent on defense contracts. The buildup to World War II set off a "blitz bloom" that doubled the region's population. But peace did not erase those gains; most people stayed and moved into affordable suburban ranch houses that covered the landscape. Freeways tied the region together and urban sprawl extended throughout the western third of the county.

In the process of growth and change, many notable landmarks fell to the bulldozer. But many others remain, restored and reused. Downtown San Diego offers a mixture of both old and new — with more change on the way. But north, south and east, the story is the same. The county population of some 3 million will grow by a third by 2020 and Tijuana to the south is expected to increase its size even faster. That means the San Diego-Tijuana region will be home to some 6 million residents early in the 21st century. At the dawn of the 20th century, the region counted less than 40,000 residents.

But something is different about the new century. The get-rich-quick crowd is far outnumbered by those who were born here or moved here for a better life and don't plan to leave. A new stability in the population means that new generations of San Diegans will have a personal link to the place and memories to pass on to their children and grandchildren. A sense of history, a shared past, is developing among many residents. They share it with their friends visiting from beyond the county borders. They defend it in the face of development pressures and often win a compromise with "progress." We hope this pictorial postcard will help both residents and visitors learn to appreciate where San Diego has come from so they can watch — and help determine — where it is going.

© GEORGE ROSS JEZEK

The Panama-California Exposition of 1915-16 filled the central mesa of Balboa Park with dreamlike buildings in the Spanish Colonial Revival style supervised by New York architect Bertram Goodhue. The mesa was linked to the west side of the park by the Cabrillo Bridge and a narrow roadway beneath it led from downtown to undeveloped Mission Valley. Downtown residents could walk directly into the park, following paths that meandered over the hilly landscape and were sited to take advantage of views to the bay and mountains.

Most exposition buildings have been reconstructed or restored and more were added for the California Pacific International Exposition in 1935-36. The round Ford Building, now the San Diego Aerospace Museum, is the most prominent remnant of the second fair. The biggest change to the park, other than the much matured landscaping, is the addition of Interstate 5 and State Route 163 that cut through the park and separated it from its neighboring downtown residential and commercial core.

Opening day at the Panama-California Exposition on January 1, 1915, witnessed thousands of San Diegans, eager to see the "magic city" of ornate palaces and lushly landscaped gardens along El Prado. The California Tower is in the distance. Electric-powered carts, called "electriquettes," are lined up for paying passengers.

Earth Day 2000 was one of many special events that continue to draw residents and tourists to the Prado.
Several of the exposition buildings have been reconstructed or replaced with other structures and uses,
starting with the Casa del Prado, right, which opened in 1971. The California Tower
remains the symbol of the park and San Diego's most recognized landmark.

The only way to get to and from Coronado in the 1920s was by ferry or by a long detour on the Silver Strand. The tallest building on the skyline was El Cortez Hotel, which opened in 1927. To the right of El Cortez is San Diego Trust & Savings Bank (with the cupola), and to its right, the John D. Spreckels Building occupied in later years by the Bank of America.

The ferries stopped running in 1969 when the San Diego-Coronado Bridge opened. The only building from the 1920s that is still in view is the John D. Spreckels Building at the far right with red tile roof. The tallest building is the Hyatt Regency San Diego. At the far left is Seaport Village, built on the site of the Coronado ferry landing.

© GEORGE ROSS JEZEK

Schooners and steamers dotted San Diego Harbor in 1903, as the area climbed out of a prolonged recession.
Photographed from the corner of Fifth Avenue and F Street, this view takes in the Santa Fe Wharf
in the distance and in the foreground at right, the Tower House apartment building.

New development obscures the downtown view of the bay from the Gaslamp Quarter. The highrise in the distance to the left is the Hyatt Regency hotel; the Meridian condominium tower is to its right. The windowless wall encloses a cinema complex at Horton Plaza shopping center, whose parking garage is concealed behind the window-filled Horton on Fourth apartments.

The foot of Fifth Avenue in 1913 was a maze of piers, docks and warehouses. Downtown founder Alonzo E. Horton built one of the piers after he acquired this property in 1867. A master plan completed in 1908 specified that industrial uses should predominate the area. However, there still was room for Kyle's Swimming Tank and other recreational facilities lining the bay.

As a result of dredging and filling, the old Horton-era docks and piers have disappeared and the San Diego Unified Port District has shifted uses to hotels, tourist facilities and recreation. This view from the San Diego Convention Center looks out on Embarcadero Marina Park, a fill project of the 1970s, made possible when the bay's ship channel was deepened.

The Santa Fe Depot, designed in the Spanish-Colonial motif of the Panama-California Exposition, was nearly completed in 1915 when the 1887 Victorian depot came tumbling down. In the era before airplanes and freeways, most people arrived in San Diego by train at this station at the foot of Broadway. They met their friends and family in the beautifully tiled waiting room or arcaded patio forecourt.

SAN DIEGO HISTORICAL SOCIETY

The depot serves Amtrak train passengers, Coaster commuters from North County and San Diego Trolley riders heading to the Mexican border, Mission Valley and East County. The forecourt, torn down to make way for a parking lot, has been replaced by a pleasant fountain and palm-rimmed plaza. The depot, still owned privately, is to be the center of hundreds of millions of dollars in condominium, office and hotel developments.

The center of downtown San Diego life had moved north to Broadway by the time this photo was taken. But 1912 saw some
momentous events near this corner of Fourth Avenue and E Street. A rally on behalf of the socialist Industrial Workers of the World
turned into a riot. Later that year, health officials raided several bordellos to rid the area of its redlight district
in advance of the 1915 Panama-California Exposition.

Named the Gaslamp Quarter in 1974, the $16\frac{1}{2}$-block nationally designated historic district sees lots of action, especially on weekend nights and during arts and music festivals throughout the year. The highrise in the distance was for many years the Watts Building, completed about 1913. It is now a timeshare hotel.

Fifth Avenue at Market Street (then known as H Street) at the height of the boom of the 1880s boasted one of the few paved streets in San Diego. This was the city's business center and it was lit at night by 100-foot-tall arc lamps, whose bulbs were changed daily. The boom collapsed in 1888, but it left behind many Victorian-style buildings, including the Backesto Block at the left and the Mercantile Building at the right. In the distance are two slender towers at the Louis Bank of Commerce Building.

Long called the Stingaree, lower Fifth Avenue became the Gaslamp Quarter in the 1970s when property owners set about restoring their century-old buildings. The Backesto Block offers light-filled offices on the second floor and restaurants and sidewalk cafes at street level. The Mercantile Building houses a home furnishings retail outlet carved out of the middle of the structure. To complement the private improvements, the city installed special period light poles and brick pavers on the sidewalks. In the distance is the downtown financial district with its high-rise office towers lining B Street.

A year after it opened in 1913, the St. James Hotel on Sixth Avenue in downtown San Diego was all set for the tourists heading to the 1915-16 Panama-California Exposition in Balboa Park. It sported a Turkish bath, a women's lounge and purportedly the fastest electric elevator in town. On the street were horse-drawn wagons and gas-powered automobiles. Nearby was the cupola-topped Hotel Majestic.

SAN DIEGO HISTORICAL SOCIETY

The St. James hotel became the Ramada Inn and Suites in 1997 and attracted a different crowd of conventioneers and tourists. Both are drawn to the surrounding Gaslamp Quarter, where many 19th century buildings have been restored. On this side of the block, no other historic buildings remain. But period light fixtures and brick pavers identify the historic district as something special.

Seen from the U.S. Grant Hotel palm court, Horton Plaza park was the center of town in 1919. The fountain and park, designed in 1910
by San Diego architect Irving J. Gill, featured stately queen palms, neatly mowed lawns and restful benches.
Two movie theaters, the Cabrillo and Plaza, were just to the south.

The plaza was restored in 1985 when the Horton Plaza shopping center opened as downtown San Diego's first major retail redevelopment effort. The dragon sits atop a former department store building now housing the Planet Hollywood restaurant and various specialty shops. The U.S. Grant's palm court has been enclosed for use as a ballroom.

El Cortez Hotel, opened in 1927, became San Diego's top place to stay with its sweeping views of the bay. In the 1950s, its new owner,
Harry Handlery, added a glass elevator and rooftop restaurant and bar, giving the hotel even more status as the place to be.
Downtown was center of the town in this pre-freeway age. Traffic was always jammed, as this scene at Sixth Avenue and B Street suggests.
Shoppers and workers competed for scarce parking spaces, while at least one person is getting along on a bicycle.
Traffic managers have yet to install one-way streets and computer-guided traffic signals.

El Cortez ended its hotel days in 1978 but hung on for the right use until 2000, when it became a posh apartment address once again (it originally housed both renters and hotel guests). Other buildings have been replaced by office towers at Sixth and B and one-way streets and synchronized traffic lights help with circulation, but there still isn't enough parking.

India Street in the Middletown district, just north of San Diego's central business district, was a thriving Italian community at the beginning of the 20th century. Tony Bernardini posed outside Tait's Meat Market at India and Cedar streets, while children looked on. A mixture of turn-of-the-century homes and two-level retail and apartment buildings lined the streets between Beech and Laurel. Tuna fishermen had easy access to their boats docked a few blocks west.

Italian businesses and restaurants still do a lively trade, even though most families have scattered throughout the San Diego area. The construction of Interstate 5 in the 1960s destroyed part of the community, while the decline of San Diego's fishing and canning industry forced Little Italy workers to find other employment. New construction has added this small hotel at the corner and new condominium and apartment developments herald renewed interest in living along India Street.

SAN DIEGO HISTORICAL SOCIETY

With Balboa Park's development for the 1915-16 Panama-California Exposition, surrounding residential communities, including South Park, took on a Spanish Colonial look inspired by the architecture at the fair. The home at 28th and A was designed by Richard Requa, who perfected what he called a "Southern California style" of white stucco walls and red-tile roofs. Requa later became the supervising architect for the second fair, the California Pacific International Exposition in 1935-36. Note that the palms trees now all tower over the houses and the streetcar lines have been replaced by cars driving on paved streets.

Looking north on 28th Street from A Street, this section of Golden Hill is also called South Park. But at the time of this 1906 photo, Balboa Park was still largely undeveloped and residences were just being built in this subdivision on the park's eastern edge. Unpaved streets made transportation difficult except by streetcar — and in those days, real estate developers could not proceed unless they could assure buyers of their lots that streetcar service was available or coming soon. Buyers erected handsome Craftsman-style homes and the subdividers put up monument markers and planted baby palm trees to convey a sense of permanence and future beauty.

Back before Prohibition, San Diego boasted a number of breweries, including the Mission Brewery and bottling plant at Washington and Hancock streets in an area of Middletown, formerly known as Five Points. Brewmasters claimed San Diego's "excellence of San Diego water" made for great beer.

© GEORGE ROSS JEZEK

With temperance gaining popularity, the brewery switched to making and bottling soft drinks. During the 1918-19 flu epidemic, it became an isolation hospital. From 1923, American Agar Co. processed seaweed at the plant to produce a variety of products. In 1985, the building was restored for professional office space. Voters approved a variance from height limits so the old chimney could be rebuilt.

To instill some culture into booming San Diego in the 1880s, a group of businessmen brought artist, musician and mystic Jesse Shepard
to town and built him this house, the Villa Montezuma at 20th and K streets. It featured stained-glass windows,
finely carved moldings and cornices and a sweeping view of the bay.

When the boom ended, Shepard left town along with thousands of other short-timers. He entertained the crowned heads of Europe but returned to America and died in poverty and obscurity in 1927. Meanwhile the Villa Montezuma remained intact and eventually was restored and became a house museum, operated by the San Diego Historical Society.

Thousands of San Diegans witnessed the dedication July 16, 1929, of the Junipero Serra Museum in Presidio Park. Designed by
William Templeton Johnson, the building was donated by George W. Marston, who also gave the park land to the city.
It was here 160 years earlier that the Franciscan friar had celebrated the first mass in San Diego
and that a presidio, or fort, was established by Spanish soldiers.

SAN DIEGO HISTORICAL SOCIETY

Because of the Depression, Marston's gift was not immediately accepted by the city and he paid to maintain the building and park for another ten years before the city took full responsibility. The San Diego Historical Society, which Marston founded in 1928, operates the building as a museum on pre-1850 San Diego. Several excavations of the presidio have unearthed thousands of artifacts, but the adobe foundations generally remain covered for protection from the elements.

Old Town's Washington Square, where American troops raised the Stars and Stripes after taking over San Diego during the Mexican-American War in 1846, was the stop in 1910 for steam-powered trains carrying passengers looking for "Ramona's Marriage Place." The building in the center background was actually the Casa de Estudillo, built for one of San Diego's most prominent Mexican families and restored after the turn of the century. Its popular name derives from the title character in Helen Hunt Jackson's landmark 1884 novel.

Old Town San Diego State Historic Park includes the Casa de Estudillo, behind the trees in the distance, as a house museum. The verdant square features landscaping that never existed during the Mexican period. Many buildings have been restored or reconstructed to reflect the period before the center of San Diego moved to downtown.

SAN DIEGO HISTORICAL SOCIETY

Mission Valley, looking west from a point just south of today's Town & Country hotel, was a peaceful farming community early in the 20th century. That is until a massive flood in January 1916 swelled the San Diego River to cover the entire valley floor.

Agricultural use continued into the 1950s, until construction of Interstate 8 and the Mission Valley Center shopping mall replaced farms with urban development. One of the few remaining large open spaces is the Riverwalk Golf Club (formerly Stardust Country Club). An alternate plan in 1958 to retain the valley as open space leading to Mission Bay Park never got off the ground.

© GEORGE ROSS JEZEK

The Franciscan friars moved Mission San Diego de Alcalá in 1774 to this location in Mission Valley to be away from soldiers at the presidio and closer to Indians living near the San Diego River. Seen in 1912 at the far left, the mission underwent various restorations starting in the 1930s, while the surrounding area remained farmland.

The mission can be barely seen amidst the urbanization. It is the red-tile and white stuccoed building directly above and slightly to the right of the yellow school bus traveling west on Interstate 8. Farms are no more as light industrial, office and retail uses fill this end of the valley.

This may look like Kansas but it was really University Avenue looking east from Georgia Street. A streetcar line was built in 1907 to serve the newly developing North Park community. A 32-foot cut into the ridge at Georgia Street opened up University Avenue property to streetcars and easy access by new residents.

SAN DIEGO HISTORICAL SOCIETY

© GEORGE ROSS JEZEK

A new bridge over University Avenue at Georgia Street was built in 1914 when the streetcar line was double tracked. But cars soon surpassed mass transit in popularity and the last streetcar was removed from service in 1949. Post-World War II growth filled in most of North Park and other neighborhoods south of Interstate 8 and single-family homes gave way in many blocks to apartment buildings.

Founded in 1897, San Diego State University was originally a two-year teachers college, located on Park Boulevard in University Heights.
With voter approval, a new campus opened in February 1931. W.K. Daniels designed the complex on otherwise undeveloped
Montezuma Mesa in a modified Spanish Colonial motif. The tower was named
for Edwin L. Hardy, who oversaw the relocation of the college.

SAN DIEGO HISTORICAL SOCIETY

Hardy Tower in the original quadrangle is obscured in this view at College Avenue and Montezuma Road. Achieving university status in 1972, the campus rose to an enrollment exceeding 30,000 at times and has embarked on a redevelopment plan for the surrounding neighborhood.

This Mission Revival house was the home of Thomas Meanley and his wife, Nackey, daughter of publisher E.W. Scripps.
At the turn of the 20th century Scripps, owner of the *San Diego Sun*, bought thousands of acres north of San Diego
for a winter retreat. His partner in the development was his half-sister, Ellen Browning Scripps.
Meanley, E.W.'s secretary, raised cattle on this 1,000-acre portion of Miramar Ranch.

Two years after Thomas M. Meanley died in 1985, his house was razed as he had requested and the land was deeded to the city of San Diego. The Scripps Ranch Library was built nearby and some artifacts from the old house, such as doors and windows, were incorporated into the design.

SAN DIEGO AEROSPACE MUSEUM

The southern tip of Point Loma in 1928 was occupied by a Coast Guard lighthouse and not much else. A lonely road led to the Cabrillo National Monument, marked by the retired 1855 lighthouse and Fort Rosecrans gunnery stations. In the distance were lightly populated North Island army and navy airfields.

The lighthouse is still active but much more development has taken place. World War II and the Cold War brought naval research stations to Point Loma. Cabrillo National Monument expanded to encompass a major visitor center. And North Island, physically joined Coronado through the filling of "Spanish Bight" in the 1940s, has a greatly expanded naval air station.

Soon after California gained statehood in 1850, Congress authorized construction of the Point Loma Lighthouse. Operated from 1855 to 1891, the facility was located on a remote, uninhabited and nearly inaccessible spot. Frequent fogs caused it to be abandoned and replaced with the present lighthouse at the water's edge.

The old lighthouse was incorporated into the Cabrillo National Monument, carved out of the military reservation that occupies the southern tip of Point Loma. Restored in recent years, the lighthouse interior depicts the lonely family life of Robert Decatur Israel, who operated the light for 20 years.

The U.S. Army Artillery District at Fort Rosecrans developed in the wake of the Spanish-American War of 1898. It included a row of duplex officers quarters constructed in 1904. The design was similar to structures at other army bases, although built in wood rather than brick as was common on the East Coast.

Now called the San Diego Submarine Base, the old fort belongs to the Navy. The duplexes are covered while they undergo structural stabilization and restoration. Other historic buildings on the base have been restored and adapted for office use. Artifacts from the base's days as an Indian settlement, Spanish fort, whaling station and American fort have been unearthed for further study and exhibition.

SAN DIEGO HISTORICAL SOCIETY

Among the many events staged at the time of the Panama-California Exposition in 1915 was a roadrace on this unpaved stretch of Chatsworth Boulevard in Point Loma. Note the streetcar cruising along a track near the present alignment of Nimitz Boulevard.

Point Loma is nearly all developed and motorists would chance getting a speeding ticket if they tried to run a race on Chatsworth now.
At right is Richard Henry Dana Junior High School, built in 1941 to accommodate San Diego's growing wartime population.

SAN DIEGO HISTORICAL SOCIETY

Bought in 1903 by sporting goods magnate Albert G. Spalding, Sunset Cliffs was a rustic, undeveloped expanse at the time of this photo.
In the distance on the hill were Katherine Tingley's dome-topped Theosophical Society school and headquarters. Spalding, one of
Tingley's backers, spent $2 million on roads, pagodas, footbridges and other improvements before his death in 1915.

Spalding's improvements and have come and gone, victims of constant erosion from the waves pounding the cliffs. To protect Sunset Cliffs Boulevard and private homes from falling into the ocean, tons of boulders were deposited at the base of the cliffs in 1971 from Ladera to Osprey streets. Meanwhile, Katherine Tingley's Homestead compound became a college campus and most of her fanciful buildings were replaced.

Visitors to boomtime San Diego in 1888 hired horse-and-buggies to take them to what was then called Mussel Beach (for the mussels harvested along the shoreline). Land speculators also brought potential lot buyers to the beach and hoped they would be captivated by the breathtaking ocean views. When the boom ended, so did the get-rich-quick schemes of both buyers and sellers.
Beachside subdivisions from Ocean Beach to Oceanside would not be fully developed for another fifty years.

Ocean Beach sports a pier and no tallyhos on its sandy shore. A condominium complex sits on the distant bluff and the summer crowds seek the best spots to surf, not mussels to eat. The community, home to hippie culture in the 1960s, still resists the upscale development of other San Diego beach communities. Foreign students mix with counterculture relics and mom-and-pop shops and restaurants thrive on business from fiercely loyal crowds.

Wonderland amusement park opened July 4, 1913. It boasted the largest roller coaster on the West Coast, a dance pavilion,
fun zone with 40 attractions, roller skating rink and children's playground. Vacant lots still predominated in the seaside community,
but until the Panama-California Exposition opened in Balboa Park two years later, this was the place to be.

Attendance at Wonderland dropped off once the exposition opened and high tides in 1916 washed away most of the buildings. The animals at the menagerie were sold to the nascent San Diego Zoological Society and Ocean Beach proceeded to develop in subsequent decades. It was a center of San Diego's "counter-culture" in the 1960s and remains a popular surfer spot. Two of the most prominent landmarks today are the steeples of Point Loma Methodist Church on the left and Sacred Heart Catholic Church on the right.

Mission Bay was undeveloped mudflats when John D. Spreckels built the Mission Beach Amusement Center on leased
city tidelands in 1925. It featured a ballroom (left), indoor plunge (right), and the Giant Dipper roller coaster.
After Spreckels' death in 1926, the city leased the property to other operators.

Now called Belmont Park, Spreckels' amusement center was redeveloped in the 1980s, but the plunge and roller coaster remained in place. A parking lot and lifeguard tower occupy the ballroom site. Mission Bay's mudflats have given way to an aquatic wonderland, made possible by extensive dredging in the 1940s and 50s. The community is home to year-round residents, although many property owners continue to welcome seasonal guests. The beach itself draws capacity crowds on a summer's day.

The Mission Beach boardwalk became an instant hit when developer John D. Spreckels opened the Mission Beach Amusement Center in 1925. Dress was far from casual, even on the beach, and uniformed sailors mingled easily with civilians.

The amusement center, now called Belmont Park, retains the Giant Dipper roller coaster and Plunge indoor swimming pool, key attractions in the early days. But present day beachgoers adhere to a more relaxed, uninhibited dress code and sailors rarely arrive in their uniforms. Bicycles and rollerblades are a favorite form of transport up and down the boardwalk.

Mission Boulevard in 1927 was divided down the middle by the Route 16 street car tracks and overhead power poles. At the left is the Strand Hotel and next to that, the Home Bake Shop and a real estate office. Extension of the San Diego Electric Railway to Mission Beach occurred at the same time as the opening of the Mission Beach Amusement Center (Belmont Park), both owned by John D. Spreckels. But as this photograph suggests, mass transit was already giving way to privately owned motorcars.

The streetcar and power poles are gone in the middle of Mission Boulevard but the Strand Hotel building still stands, its ground floor occupied by a restaurant. The community retains its low-scale profile thanks to a 1972 city ballot initiative and statewide coastal-protection measure that imposed heights limits in the coastal zone throughout California.

Earl Taylor, who moved to Pacific Beach in 1923 and began developing lots, encouraged Neil Nettleship to build a pier as he and his associates had done in Santa Monica and Venice beach. The 950-foot-long pier dedicated April 18, 1926 had carnival concessions and a ballroom (10-cent admission and 5 cents per dance). But within three months, Nettleship discovered the contractors had not protected the pilings against erosion and the property was condemned and foreclosed.

In 1935, ten motel cottages were added, the pilings were replaced and the pier reopened in 1936. A storm in 1983 destroyed 150 feet of decking and restoration began two years later. The pier office building, housing five hotel suites and a hotel room, was proposed to be razed in the early-1990s but it was preserved and the owner added six new cottages and spruced up the property.

SAN DIEGO HISTORICAL SOCIETY

This 1927 view of Pacific Beach looking south demonstrates how undeveloped even San Diego's ocean-close neighborhoods remained in the years following World War I. Mission Bay was an undeveloped wildlife habitat, its islets visited only by bird life and duck hunters.

The old-fashioned street light standards are about the only link to the past. The 1920s buildings sites are all occupied.
Mission Bay is an aquatic wonderland and wildlife has migrated elsewhere.

La Jolla Properties Company began developing the La Jolla Hermosa tract in 1924. The subdivision, like many others, was advertised as an "exclusive" neighborhood, "San Diego's socially correct spot to live." The La Jolla Hermosa station, designed by Eugene M. Hoffman and opened in 1925, was patterned after the San Carlos de Boromeo mission in Carmel.

The hills have filled in with homes and the San Carlos streetcar station has become the La Jolla United Methodist Church. Vans, not horsedrawn wagons, transport goods. But other things haven't changed, such as the presence of palm trees dotting the landscape.

SAN DIEGO HISTORICAL SOCIETY

Cows, yes, cows were a stone's throw from the newly opened La Jolla High School in 1924. Fay Avenue was unpaved and there were no houses in sight. But this scene was soon to change as development picked up steam in the Roaring Twenties.

Porsches, eucalyptus trees, utility poles and hillside homes now can be seen on Fay Avenue. A fence encloses La Jolla High's football field and nearly every lot has been developed. One of San Diego's most expensive neighborhoods, La Jolla is not all mansions and million-dollar views. There are retirement homes, small two-bedroom houses and an assortment of mom-and-pop shops and restaurants.

SAN DIEGO HISTORICAL SOCIETY

Beautiful homes now occupy La Jolla Shores and
the Scripps complex has been vastly expanded.
The prominent architecture of La Jolla
is stucco and red-tile roofed Spanish Colonial
or California Mission. But the ocean
is still as blue as ever.

A jewel in the rough, La Jolla Shores in 1917 was barely accessible and virtually undeveloped. The only significant improvements were the pier and buildings at Scripps Institution of Oceanography at the far north end. In downtown La Jolla, substantial year-round homes filled many blocks overlooking the shore.

A popular artist's colony in the 1890s, La Jolla was a four-hour trip from San Diego before street cars and automobiles arrived.
The post-World War I period saw La Jolla Cove become a popular weekend and summer swimming spot,
as this photo suggests. The most prominent building overlooking the cove is the Joseph Rodes beach cottage,
which a later owner called the Brockton Villa in honor of her Massachusetts hometown.

The coastline is virtually unchanged but the vacant land has been covered with homes, hotels and an occasional high-rise development. The Brockton Villa, now dwarfed by its neighbor, became a restaurant in 1990. Another historic building, the red-colored 1894 Red Rest cottage at the far right, sits abandoned, its owners hoping to replace it with a new development.

Opened on Prospect Street in 1913, the Colonial Hotel was enlarged in 1928, with the construction of a four-story, concrete apartment hotel that was designed by Frank Richardson. Owners A. B. Harlan and George Bane derived the name from two white pillars on either side of the front door on the original wood-frame building, relocated to the rear of the property.

The La Jolla Drug Store was part of the old and enlarged hotel from 1915 onwards and the pharmacist's son, Gregory Peck, visited the hotel while he performed at the summer La Jolla Playhouse. Now called the Grande Colonial Hotel, the building has been upgraded and renovated. Gone are the rooftop sign and drugstore. But the hotel's restaurant, Putnam's, commemorates the pharmacy's one-time owner, Silas O. Putnam, who added an ever-popular ice cream parlor on the sidewalk.

After La Jolla's first golf course, established in 1899 at Prospect and Cave streets, was developed for homes starting about 1910, a nine-hole course was set up on the western slope of Mount Soledad. The La Jolla Land and Improvement Company, established in 1921, raised $30,000 to make a permanent 18-hole course. The $25,000 clubhouse, designed by Herbert Mann, was dedicated in 1927.

La Jolla Country Club, like many other institutions, suffered from financial difficulties during the Depression, but recovered with restructuring of $181,000 in debt. Today the club, with about 450 members, still occupies a view-packed location surrounded by beautiful spacious homes.

Established by marine biologist William Ritter, Scripps Institution of Oceanography became part of the University of California in 1912 and occupied buildings funded largely by publisher E.W. Scripps and his half-sister, Ellen Browning Scripps. The first permanent building was named the George Scripps building, after Ellen's half-brother who died prematurely. It was designed by San Diego's leading architect, Irving J. Gill, and featured many elements conducive to scientific work. Most of the staff, including director Ritter, lived at the research station since there was no private housing nearby and transportation to La Jolla was difficult.

Scripps Institution of Oceanography became the nucleus of the University of California, San Diego, which welcomed its first undergraduates in 1964 on nearby Torrey Pines Mesa. The oceanography departments now occupy many buildings and no one lives on site, although some of the earliest dwellings remain. Expensive homes fill the La Jolla Shores community that abuts the university land and downtown La Jolla is only minutes away by car. The latest Scripps Pier was built in 1987.

Established as a city park in 1899, Torrey Pines State Reserve south of Del Mar is the only spot where the rare Torrey pine grows
naturally other than on Santa Rosa Island, 175 miles away off the coast of Santa Barbara. This view, taken from the reserve looking north,
encompasses the undeveloped section of Del Mar Terrace where roads were laid but no houses were built.
The Santa Fe Railroad line cut diagonally across the valley, heading toward Sorrento Valley
in an inland jog around Mount Soledad.

The natural landscape has not changed greatly and the Torrey pines remain protected. But the northern slopes overlooking Peñasquitos River Valley have filled in with homes and condominiums. Trains continue crossing the valley floor, but off to the right and out of view is the much congested merge of Interstates 5 and 805, built in the 1960s and 70s.

The budding flower-growing community of Carlsbad, which also billed itself as the "Natural Home of the Avocado,"
boasted a lively commercial district centered on State and Elm. Carlsbad National Bank was on one corner
and Mark Coffin's lumberyard was at another. Up the street were the Carlsbad Theater and Los Diego Hotel.
The poshest place in town was Carlsbad Mineral Springs resort two blocks
to the west on recently paved Carlsbad Boulevard.

The center of town shifted to Carlsbad Boulevard as it became the quicker route between San Diego and Los Angeles. Hollywood actors and producers discovered Carlsbad and Leo Carrillo, the "Cisco Kid," bought a 1,600 acre ranch east of El Camino Real. Interstate 5's construction in the 1960s split downtown down the middle, but officials acted to revitalize the area with special architectural and landscaping controls.

Three years after it opened in 1909, the Del Mar train station was one of a handful of brick depots built by the Atchison, Topeka & Santa Fe Railway before a revival in Spanish Colonial architecture shifted designs to stucco and tile. In the distance, Del Mar's beachfront property was virtually undeveloped. The Stratford Inn Garage served patrons of the nearby hotel.

The Coaster commuter train passes the Del Mar station without stopping, local service having ceased in 1995 for both train riders and commuters. The hills of distant Solana Beach, where the trains now stop, are covered with homes and Del Mar's beach property has shifted from seasonal use to year-round residences.

The San Dieguito River Valley, as seen looking south, was once planted in lima beans and sugar beets. But a disastrous flood inundated
the fields, destroying their agricultural potential. The Santa Fe Land and Improvement Company built Lake Hodges Dam in 1918
to control flooding and the valley once again became useful, this time for cattle grazing,
honeycomb manufacturing and other purposes.

The destiny of the San Dieguito River Valley took a completely different turn in 1936, when the 22nd District Agricultural Association bought 241 acres on which to build a county fairgrounds. The Del Mar Racetrack opened in 1937 and has held annual meets ever since. During World War II, the racetrack was taken over by Camp Pendleton Marines, who staged amphibious landing exercises. To the southeast was a naval blimp base, which after the war became a county air strip until 1959, the year Del Mar incorporated.

SAN DIEGO HISTORICAL SOCIETY

The town of Encinitas ("little oaks") came into existence in 1883 when rail service was extended to San Diego County. After the turn of the century, flower growing became the community's most famous business. In 1912, a lonely farmhouse occupied a bluff at Encinitas' Moonlight Beach. During Prohibition in the 1920s, the beach became a beachhead for bootleggers, who landed gallons of straight alcohol for shipment to illegal speakeasies.

The rural life is long gone in present-day Encinitas. Moonlight State Beach is a popular surfing spot and expensive homes and condominiums occupy its bluffs. Leucadia, Cardiff-by-the-Sea, Olivenhain and Encinitas joined in 1986 to incorporate as the city of Encinitas and control their own growth. Flower fields became residential communities and prices skyrocketed as San Diegans sought homes near the ocean.

The marquee on La Paloma, Encinitas' movie palace, advertised a Laurel and Hardy comedy, along with news reels, in this 1929 view.
The $50,000 theater had opened a year earlier and featured a $14,000 pipe organ. The First Street location made for
maximum exposure for motorists passing through town on U.S. Highway 101,
the main north-south link from Los Angeles to San Diego.

Encinitas, like many coastal communities, lost business when Interstate 5 replaced Highway 101 in the 1960s. La Paloma, closed for a decade in 1963 and underwent a major restoration in the 1990s. Meanwhile, Encinitas incorporated in 1986 and included the neighboring towns of Cardiff-by-the-Sea, Leucadia and Olivenhain.

On a knoll at the east end of Grand Avenue in 1906 stood the 100-room Escondido Hotel. Completed in 1886, its opening coincided with the real estate boom in Southern California caused by the arrival of railway service from the east. The city was incorporated in 1888 and at the time of this 1906 photo had a population of 755. The building at the far right was the Steiner & Co. general merchandise store.

Escondido's downtown at Grand Avenue and Broadway looks nothing like it did a century ago. The hotel, torn down in 1925, has been replaced by the Palomar Medical Center. Steiner & Co. and virtually all other businesses have turned over. But the city of more than 125,000 has paved streets, extensive landscaping, a modern city hall and performing arts center.

Julian was a peaceful mountain village in 1884 with only about 100 inhabitants. Its Main Street was hardly a bustling highway to anywhere.
But in the winter of 1869-70, Frederick Coleman, an African-American who built and operated toll roads, discovered gold.
Julian grew nearly as big as San Diego as fortune seekers dashed into the mountains.

The gold rush didn't last long, but another kind of rush eventually replaced it: apples. Each fall so many tourists visit Julian to sample homemade apple pie that local bakers have to import extra fruit to meet the demand. Antique shops, bed-and-breakfast hotels and other attractions make for a year-round festive mood in this mountain community.

SAN DIEGO HISTORICAL SOCIETY

Oceanside voters approved a $100,000 bond issue in 1926 to build its fourth pier (pictured here in 1929). An estimated 20,000 people from all over Southern California attended a three-day celebration of the 1,900-foot pier. The Strand was paved at this time and visitors set up summer campsites on the beach and called it Tent City. Cecil B. DeMille filmed several movies in the Oceanside area and film stars also were reported camping or sunbathing near the pier.

The ocean has not been kind to Oceanside's pier over the years. The 1927 pier was buffeted by winter storms with major damage occurring in 1942. Voters approved $175,000 in bonds in 1946 and the replacement opened in 1947. In 1976 and 1978, storms struck again and the pier was reduced to only 1,000 feet in length. A $5 million replacement opened in 1987.

SAN DIEGO HISTORICAL SOCIETY

The Franciscan order established 21 missions in Alta (Upper) California from 1769 to 1823. The first was Mission San Diego de Alcalá and in 1798 a second mission in the area opened in what is today the city of Oceanside. The Mission San Luis Rey honors French King Louis IX (1226-1270), considered one of medieval Europe's most chivalrous monarchs. This "king of the missions," a century after its construction, was still surrounded by farmlands and few residences. Unlike many other missions in the chain, it was still in relatively good physical condition.

Mission San Luis Rey has undergone extensive renovations in the last century but, as this photograph demonstrates, it is no longer surrounded by farmlands. Suburban tract homes encroach in all directions and traffic noise interrupts the calm around the mission grounds.

This stone-faced heap at the foot of Mount Woodson outside Ramona was the brainchild of Amy Strong, San Diego's turn-of-the-century seamstress to the wealthy. She hired Emmor Brooke Weaver and John Vawter to design what became a 27-room Craftsman villa. Among its eccentricities was a windmill, inspired by Strong's visit to the Netherlands on one of her many European buying trips.

In 1991, the development of the 380-acre Mount Woodson residential subdivision prompted builder William Davidson to incorporate the Amy Strong "castle" into his 189-home golf-course community. The building was added to the National Register of Historic Places in 1978.

Looking northeast along Avenida Delicias, early visitors to Rancho Santa Fe could stay at La Morada, a 12-room guesthouse designed by
Lilian Rice, who did other major design work for the community's masterplan developer,
the Santa Fe Land and Improvement Company.

Now called The Inn at Rancho Santa Fe, the property has expanded to 89 rooms but retains the same quiet, rustic character of its origin.
The view to Paseo Delicias remains virtually unchanged, except for the mature landscaping. Steve Royce,
a former New York Giants pitcher, bought the hotel in 1958 and his family still controls it.
Meanwhile, Rancho Santa Fe has grown into San Diego's premier residential community.

Located between Del Mar and Rancho Santa Fe, Fairbanks Ranch was bought by Douglas Fairbanks Jr. and Mary Pickford in 1926
as a retreat from their high-profile lives in Hollywood. They called it Rancho Zorro after Fairbanks' movie, "The Mark of Zorro."
They planted several thousand citrus trees and acres of beans, tomatoes and grain to feed some 250 head of cattle which roamed the area.
The seven-acre lake was created in 1928 and the couple planned a spacious hacienda to be designed by Wallace Neff.
But their divorce in the year this photo was taken halted such plans.

Fairbanks Ranch today appeals even more to the privacy-seeking wealthy, who live in gated communities and engage in golfing, horseback riding and other pursuits. Near the ranch was the site of the equestrian competition during the 1984 summer Olympics, held in Los Angeles. The racecourse then became the Fairbanks Ranch Country Club. Ranch developer Ray Watt based his home on the hacienda Fairbanks and Pickford never built.

SAN DIEGO HISTORICAL SOCIETY

When Ed Fletcher bought the former Lockwood Mesa in 1923, he changed the name to Solana Beach and changed the landscape. He immediately embarked on a three-month hydroblasting project to create a direct route from the cliff to the beach.

Renamed Fletcher Cove in 1987, the Fletcher cut continues to be a popular access point to the beach. Solana Beach incorporated as a city in 1986 at the same time as its neighbor, Encinitas. The community of about 15,000 now boasts a creative visual arts community along Cedros Avenue and welcomes Coaster commuters at its modern train station.

115

Incorporated in 1911, Chula Vista had a population of 500 and a downtown of muddy streets, horse-and-buggies, streetcars and
a respectable number of automobiles. At the corner of Third Avenue and F Street in this 1912 photo was the Chula Vista State Bank.
The next year, voters approved installing 26 street lights and paving some of the streets.
But for many decades, citrus orchards remained a prime source of income for residents.

After World War II, Chula Vista turned its lemon groves into tract home building sites. The city grew to a population at century's end of about 175,000, the county's second largest. The ARCO Olympic Training Center and Coors Amphitheater opened in the 1990s and the giant Otay Ranch began its conversion from farmland to subdivisions. Meanwhile, at Third and F, downtown revitalization and beautification introduced street trees, architectural controls and special paving materials.

Formed in 1897, the San Diego Country Club operated a golf course in Balboa Park until 1913, when it moved to Loma Portal and joined the Point Loma Golf Club, established by sports industrialist and land developer A.G. Spalding. By the time of this photograph, the club had moved to a 160-acre site in Chula Vista. James Simpson was the first head pro and in the 1930s the going rate was $1 per round and $9 per month dues.

The San Diego Country Club has hosted many tournaments and champions, including Gene Sarazen, Lee Trevino and Ben Hogan. The first San Diego Open occurred in 1952. The 1964 U.S. Women's Open was won by Mickey Wright. The 6,631-yard course is enjoyed by 500 members and eight annual charity tournaments. The current clubhouse was completed in 1989.

To appeal to a wide variety of guests in 1900, Hotel Del Coronado owner John D. Spreckels established Tent City south of the hotel for summer guests. Served by Spreckels' streetcar system, visitors enjoyed basic accommodations. Entertainment for the 1909 season featured a "Colored Rag Time Band - 10 Artists." In the distance to the left was a pier, and at the right, the Coronado Boat House. Both men and women and their children maintained a rather formal dress code.

The hotel and boat house are still in view but Tent City ceased operations in 1939. Coronado Shores condominium towers were built on the campsite in the 1970s, approved before coastal height limitations became effective. Reliance on the streetcar gave way to cars, although residents and visitors do enjoy bike riding on Coronado's flat streets. The vacant land along Glorietta Bay seen here is a proposed site for a new city hall complex.

SAN DIEGO HISTORICAL SOCIETY

Many 19th century hotels disappeared in the
20th century, but not the Hotel Del. Its owners
maintained and modernized it over the decades.
The house-like structure was removed in 1932.
In recent decades, new rooms and
meeting facilities have been added.

The Hotel Del Coronado in 1900 beckoned
winter guests, who stayed for months at a time.
Guests took ferries and streetcars to the hotel,
so that much of the grounds could remain
lushly landscaped. Hotel owner John D. Spreckels
authorized $50,000 in renovations,
including 87 new bathrooms.
The house-like structure was an office,
possibly for the hotel physician.

In 1909, the Imperial Beach Improvement Association built a 500-foot pier at the foot of Elm Avenue. The Edwards Wave Motor Co. spent about two years trying to generate electricity from wave action before removing its equipment.

After heavy winter storms in 1951-52 destroyed the old pier, a 900-foot replacement at the foot of Evergreen Avenue was built in 1962. It also fell victim to storm damage in 1983-85 and was replaced on the same site with a 1,200-foot pier that was somewhat wider and higher. Imperial Beach residents and visitors continue to enjoy the wide sandy expanse, playing volleyball or building sandcastles at an annual tournament.

B.G.PECK
REAL ESTATE
▲ LOANS AND
FIRE INSURANCE

In 1888, National City prided itself on being the terminus of the Atchison, Topeka & Santa Fe Railway. Promoted by city founder Frank A. Kimball, the railroad's promise of growth led to much development, including this length of rowhouses known as Brick Row, on A Avenue between Ninth and 10th streets.

The railroad relocated its terminus to Riverside County about the time the 1888 photo was taken. But Brick Row remained in place and underwent extensive restoration a century later. It symbolizes deep pride in National City's heritage, where other historic homes and structures have been preserved.

Elisha S. Babcock, co-developer of the Hotel Del Coronado, formed the Otay Water Co. in 1886 and, with backing from John D. Spreckels, built the Lower Otay Dam in 1897. Seen here in 1901, the dam incorporated an unusual design by Babcock, who was not an engineer.

The city of San Diego bought the dam from Spreckels in 1912 only to see it crumble in the devastating floods of January 1916. It was rebuilt in 1917-18 with a 13-billion-gallon capacity. Today, it doubles as a popular recreational reservoir and site for rowing crews at the nearby ARCO Olympic Training Center.

SAN DIEGO HISTORICAL SOCIETY

Completed in 1888, Sweetwater Dam in Spring Valley was developed by the San Diego Land and Town Co., a Santa Fe Railway entity, to serve South Bay communities. At 90 feet, it was the nation's tallest masonry dam. But it suffered damage in the 1916 flood and was reconstructed with a new spillway as this photo indicates.

The strengthened dam suffered little damage in another major flood in 1927. The Sweetwater Water Co. became the California Water & Telephone Co. in 1935 and it expanded South Bay water storage capacity with construction of the Loveland Dam 18 miles upstream near Alpine in 1945. The Sweetwater Authority, created in 1977 by the South Bay Irrigation District and National City, now operates both facilities.

Mexicans and Americans crossed the international border unobstructed and unchecked until the first U.S. Customs House was established at a general store about 1871; Mexican authorities added a customs post in 1874. A short-lived gold rush in 1889 prompted the establishment of Tijuana and tourism picked up when a racetrack opened in 1916. But the border and Tijuana gained true fame starting about the time of this photo, when Prohibition prompted thousands of Americans to go south for a drink, gambling or a bit of vice. To curb the excess, a 6 p.m. border curfew was imposed from 1926 to 1936.

World War II saw a huge increase in border crossings, both by Americans seeking goods that were not rationed and Mexicans participating in the bracero agricultural guest worker program. In recent decades, periodic crackdowns on crime, drug traffic, juvenile delinquency and other problems have occasionally disrupted the border flow. But today, the San Ysidro-Tijuana crossing is the busiest in the world, clocking more than 25 million pedestrians and motorists annually. The border was closed only once — for 19 hours in 1963 after the assassination of President John F. Kennedy, when authorities feared that the perpetrators might be trying to escape from the United States.

Viewed from Mount Helix, the El Cajon Valley was one of San Diego County's premier agricultural communities. Farmers owed the abundance to imported water brought to the valley by a 35-mile-long flume, an aqueduct completed in 1889. But a 20-year real estate bust followed the land boom of the 1880s and valley residents found themselves land poor. Still, local farmers proudly exhibited their produce at the 1893 World's Columbian Exposition in Chicago. By 1912 both El Cajon and neighboring La Mesa were stable enough to incorporate as cities.

El Cajon, which counted only 5,400 residents in 1950, ballooned to 52,300 by 1970 and nearly 100,000 by 2000. The major factor was the construction of Interstate 8 and other freeways into East County. A group of teenagers delayed the opening of I-8 a few hours by diverting traffic off to Old Highway 80 so they could run a drag strip one Friday night, but police soon ended the prank.

Looking east from La Mesa, Grossmont, left, and Mount Helix, right, were in the countryside in 1927. Grossmont, named in 1902 by developer Ed Fletcher for his partner, actor William Gross, attracted artists such as opera singer Ernestine Schumann-Heink. Mount Helix got its name in 1872 from Rufus King Porter in recognition of the rare *Helix aspersa* snails found in the area. Starting in 1917, the San Diego Ad Club began sponsoring Easter sunrise services on the mountain and a permanent outdoor theater and cross were erected in 1925. The Mount Helix Lake reservoir lies between the two hills.

Suburbanization after World War II reached the area, accelerated in the 1950s and '60s by the construction of Interstate 8 and State Route 94. Grossmont became the name of a shopping center located north of the freeway and Mount Helix became a popular building site for custom homes. However, the rural setting was marred by traffic noise and air pollution rising from the El Cajon Valley. And in the 1990s, controversy erupted over the legality of the cross on publicly owned land atop Mount Helix.

SAN DIEGO HISTORICAL SOCIETY

On the shore of Lindo Lake, one block east of downtown Lakeside, once stood the posh 80-room Lakeside Inn. Called the "Coronado of the Hills," the inn was popular with golfers and duck hunters who paid $2 per night for lodging. In 1907 at the Lakeside track, Barney Oldfield set a world record of one mile in 51.8 seconds in his Green Dragon car.

The Lakeside Inn is gone, torn down in 1920, and so is the speedway. Lakeside is still unincorporated but full of history and interesting buildings. Lindo Lake nearly dried up when the creeks feeding it were dammed or diverted. In 1997, a 200-foot well was tapped next to the lake to fill it once again.

James A. Murray, seen here at the dam he and Ed Fletcher built in 1918 creating Lake Murray, was a copper-mining tycoon from Montana. An earthen dam had been completed on the site in 1895 and the two developers replaced it with a dam that was 112 feet high and 817 feet wide. Murray died in 1921 and Fletcher went on to develop other water and transportation resources in connection with his many real estate interests.

© GEORGE ROSS JEZEK

Lake Murray looks much as it did when completed. Stocked with fish, the 150-acre reservoir continues to act as a key reservoir for San Diego's drinking water. Located within Mission Trails Regional Park, it is enjoyed by residents in the surrounding communities of Del Cerro, San Carlos and La Mesa.

SAN DIEGO HISTORICAL SOCIETY

Looking north from the Santee Public School, Mission Gorge Road meets Magnolia Avenue at the right. The most prominent building
on Magnolia was the Methodist Episcopal Church and beyond that, among the trees, the Edgemoor Dairy Farm.
The two-story building at the right was the Casa de Santee hotel and the largest building on the south side
of Mission Gorge, a general store, run by postmaster Frank B. Holder.

© GEORGE ROSS JEZEK

Virtually all of historic Santee is gone. One relic is the polo barn built at the Edgemoor Dairy Farm, where a county geriatric hospital is located. The hotel was relocated to nearby Bostonia and the church was expanded using some of the earlier structure. The center of town is now filled with assorted retail outlets and businesses. Although trains no longer pass through town, the San Diego Trolley's East line terminates at Mission Gorge and Cuyamaca Street, about a half-mile to the west.

The publisher would like to thank the following individuals and organizations who helped make this book possible.

George M. Jezek, Sr.

Roger M. Showley

Zach A. Johnson

Ronda Millward

Justin Mink

Suzanne and Steve Arriaga

John and Lois Jesek

Greg Williams

Carol Myers

Chris Travers

Cindy Kimmel

Sally West

John Panter

Dennis Sharp

Aerospace Museum

San Diego Historical Society

La Jolla Historical Society

Santee Historical Society

Oceanside Historical Society

San Diego Public Library

Union-Tribune Publishing Co.

City of San Diego

Mike Kedzior

Mark Stone

My Friends at S.D.P.D.

John Neeb

Bill Glassman

City of Del Mar

California State Parks

City of National City

Karl Godenschwager

City of Imperial Beach

Cabrillo National Monument

San Diego Hospice

San Diego Submarine Base

Prudential Real Estate

Fairbanks Ranch Association

David J. Abrams

U.S. Grant Hotel

Norm J. Wilt

Fuji Film USA

Chrome Inc.

San Diego Convention Center

San Diego Unified Port District

Kurt Christensen

Ramada Inn and Suites

Classic Reprographics

Tammy Denneson

City of Coronado

El Cortez Hotel

Hyatt Regency, San Diego

San Diego State University

Scripps Ranch Library

Crystal Pier

Grande Colonial Hotel

City of Carlsbad

City of Encinitas

City of La Mesa

U.S. Customs

Sweetwater Authority

Hotel Del Coronado

San Diego Country Club

City of Oceanside

(Next Page)

Pacific Beach • South from Crystal Pier

Multistory condominium buildings and apartments
now line the beach frontage. To aid access and
arrest erosion, a massive sea wall covers the cliff face.
This winter view shows that beach goers can still
enjoy a relatively warm San Diego day, even in January.

Photography: © George Ross Jezek